EDGE OF HOPE

The Rohingya Refugee Camp at Cox's Bazar

Photography
DAWTON & McFARLANE

ACKNOWLEDGEMENTS

We must acknowledge and thank those who inspired, helped and supported the Edge of Hope project:

Sabrina Islam whose idea it was to go and photograph the Rohingya. Esrat Karim, head of AMAL and her dedicated team, whose commitment to looking after those less fortunate in her country whether they be Bangladesh or Rohingya was both humbling and inspiring. Estiak Prottoy for his help and support throughout the duration of our time in Bangladesh. Anna Wolf for giving our photographs structure and context. Mitsuno Shibata for organising fundraising exhibitions of our work. David Asker of ImageBox Group for the wonderful exhibition prints and Faiza Meyassar Alireza whose kindness, support and generosity is the chemistry that has made this project possible.

Published by Pallas Athene (Publishers) Ltd
2 Birch Close, London N19 5XD
pallasathene.co.uk

First published 2023

Photography
© Anthony Dawton, Jim McFarlane 2023
Dawton & McFarlane – Photographic Works
dawtonmcfarlane@gmail.com
dawtonmcfarlane.com

Text
© Anthony Dawton, Jim McFarlane 2023
Introduction © Kaamil Ahmed 2023

Text quotations from *I Feel No Peace, Rohingya Fleeing Over Seas and Rivers* — By Kaamil Ahmed
Reproduced with permission from Hurst Publishers

ISBN 9781843682400

Design by Anna Wolf

Printed in Lebanon by
Kutub Publishing
kutubltd.com

There is a certain way the sun illuminates the room whenever you sit with the Rohingya in their shelters in Cox's Bazar, Bangladesh. The shade created by that piece of tarpaulin tied to a bamboo frame is broken by sunlight that can enter only through a single door frame. A few beams of light can occasionally intrude through gaps in the bamboo weaving. Many times, I have sat by the entrance of one of these Rohingya homes and been struck by the way that light falls on the face of the person I am listening to — a person made a refugee by the genocidal massacres of the Myanmar military.

So, for me, there's something very familiar about these photos taken by Anthony Dawton and Jim McFarlane, many of them in and around the shelters that comprise the world's largest refugee settlement. Almost a million people live in this network of similar camps, all built by people who escaped extreme violence. The Rohingya are a minority group from Myanmar's Rakhine state but after decades of genocide, culminating in a brutal military operation that expelled 700,000 of them in 2017, far more now live in Bangladesh's refugee camps. They arrived by boat, across the River Naf, or on foot, through fields still sodden after the monsoon season and made more unstable by the sheer number of feet trudging over them.

These camps were carved from the Bangladeshi hillsides as the Rohingya arrived, exhausted and traumatised, with nowhere to go. Forests were transformed into human settlements so rapidly that elephants that had traditionally migrated through those forests became confused, causing terrifying new encounters for the refugees. But eventually they settled in their new homes of tarpaulin and bamboo. Their shelters are rudimentary, almost identical from the outside and similarly filled with goods carrying the logos of the UN and other non-government organisations, but each with its own character inside. Somehow, they are made into homes. In the early days the camps had a dusty and desolate appearance, but the refugees began using the bamboo frames of their shelters to grow vegetables that provide nutrition, shade and some greenery. The bamboo structures double as storage places, with clothes and books wedged into gaps to keep them off the ground. A few lengths of rope can be especially useful — tied to planks of wood to create floating shelves for cooking utensils, or attached to hand-made cradles for young babies that can be gently rocked. Stacks of firewood are left on the roof outside to dry and weigh down the tarpaulin that always seems at risk of blowing away when a strong wind blows. There may not be much space, but every bit of it is used innovatively.

The Rohingya are resilient. These innovations keep their belongings off the ground when rain waters intrude. During storm seasons they dig up the earth from the surrounding area and slap it on the outside of their shelters to protect them from monsoons and cyclones. They craft any defence they can find against the constant cycle of threats from floods, storms and fires, from which they have very little protection.

A fire that starts in one shelter can rapidly spread and burn through the homes of thousands within an hour. The Rohingya in Bangladesh live in a settlement that was designed to be temporary but, in reality, appears to be a permanent home. The Rohingya have turned to Bangladesh for safety on numerous occasions in the past, most notably in 1978 and then the 1990s. Those who arrived then thought it would be temporary as well. But Myanmar has only become more dangerous for them and so they are left with nowhere else to go. Many remained in the 1990s, in the same camps that exist now, and those who were repatriated then ended up returning in 2017. No other country takes them in, and the world does little to pressure Myanmar to make their real homes safe.

I first visited the Rohingya refugee camps in Cox's Bazar in 2015 but when I returned two years later, they were unrecognisable, transformed from small settlements among the greenery to a city-like mass that had swallowed the forest.

It is telling that many of the subjects of the photos in this book are children. Throughout the camps there is a prevailing fear of a "lost generation" — who have grown up in exile, without a real education and deprived of any hope, and who will watch the world pass by as they languish in this city of tents.

In the years that I have reported from the refugee camps, I have met children shortly after their births who are now ready for their early years of schooling. Older children who would have been in secondary school, but were denied this opportunity in the refugee camps, should now be graduating and going to colleges and universities. Instead, most young people are left idle. Girls often end up in early marriages and boys are faced with a frustrating search for labouring jobs, despite being banned from work by the authorities.

Throughout the camps there is a prevailing fear of a "lost generation" — who have grown up in exile, without a real education and deprived of any hope.

Again, there are lessons to be taken from those Rohingya who have spent 30 years living in Bangladesh. Deprived of education, work and the freedom to move, hope is hard to come by, which makes the youth desperate to escape.

Many Rohingya fear their social structures are breaking down inside the camps — domestic violence increases, and young men are enticed into criminal activity out of desperation. A hunger for something more hopeful beyond the camps also makes many of the youth susceptible to the promises of human traffickers, who tell them they can find better lives in places such as Malaysia. The number of Rohingya boarding boats to South-East Asia grew 360% in 2022 but the increase in boat journeys was accompanied by an increase in the number of Rohingya dying at sea.

In 2017, the sheer brutality of the Myanmar military's massacres jolted the world to attention, forcing it to see the result of decades of violence and persecution against the minority. Journalists, photographers, aid workers and diplomats all rushed in to document and help. That interest has faded away, but the Rohingya remain. They are rarely now in the news and there is little serious talk of any change in Myanmar that would allow their return — certainly nothing that would require the international community to act. Aid has been steadily reduced and in 2023, the World Food Programme has twice cut food rations, bringing them down from $12 to $8 per person each month.

Myanmar is no safer than before. A military coup in 2021 has made it a much more dangerous place for the whole population but the continuing danger to the refugees was highlighted by Cyclone Mocha, when hundreds of Rohingya died because they were not allowed to leave the displacement camps to which they have been confined since being turfed out of their homes during the 2012 anti-Rohingya riots in Sittwe.

The photographs in this book are important; they are a reminder that the Rohingya remain in Bangladesh and must be remembered. They may not face the same imminent and extreme violence there that they would in Myanmar, but life is drained from them on a daily basis in camps that are not fit to hold a whole nation forever. Until the world acts, they will go about their lives trying to survive, making do with the fragile shelters that are now their only homes, collecting water from the wells they have drilled and watching their children grow, hoping that this generation will one day be given some reason to hope.

Kaamil Ahmed, author of *I Feel No Peace: Rohingya Fleeing Over Seas and Rivers.*

INTRODUCTION

DAWTON & McFARLANE

It is not our job as photographers to make political or geo-political comments or to offer advice or criticise NGOs or governments. We are not photo-journalists, even though wherever we have gone, more by luck than intent, we have found ourselves at the epicentre of conflicts that have marked the biggest failures of our leaders and caused misery and unwanted reverberations way beyond the land that is being fought over. Whether it is the mindless violence of the Syrian conflict or the never-ending Palestinian-Israeli struggle, these conflicts take away the potential and the hopes of thousands of people from generation to generation. These people, these families, are born into lives of zero possibilities. It is a cruelty unimaginable to us who are free to pursue our chosen courses in life.

Knowing this, it is the greatest surprise that when we go into the refugee camps or the bombed towns and villages to take photographs we find an integrity, a strength, and a nobility among refugees, and it proved true again, perhaps more so than anywhere, among the Rohingya.

Entering the Rohingya refugee camp is a sobering and extraordinary experience. There are more than 900,000 people, making it the largest refugee camp in the world, a fact that became self-evident as we walked around the crowded streets framed on either side by the makeshift bamboo huts where the Rohingya cook, live and sleep. Of those 900,000 refugees, more than 60% are children and here lies a very large problem waiting to arise. There are few schools or youth activities and soon these children will become teenagers, inactive, bored and with little educational skills. It is concerning.

It is oppressively hot sitting on the earth floor of the huts talking to families and taking their photographs. As the day comes to an end, the return to our hotel beckons but there has been a transformation in us and, although we are exhausted and our shirts are soaked through, we do not want to leave. We want to go on talking and photographing because we have recognised again the humanity of a people who have nothing but will not give up.

The Rohingya have been the victims of persecution for more than a century, and recently of genocide, and now reside in a country that tolerates them but is not ready to grant them the citizenship that would offer hope for a decent future.

There is all this history in the talk and in the faces of these stateless people, that dignity, that nobility, that care for family and for each other. It is the extraordinary result of a people dealt the very worst cards, who have nothing but their humanity.

It is electrifying to experience, and it doubled our determination to capture this triumph of spirit with our cameras and to point out the potential, the possibilities, the contribution that could be realised if the Rohingya people were 'released'. There is hope, but it is on the edge.

Dawton & McFarlane — Photographic Works
dawtonmcfarlane.com

EDGE
OF
HOPE

No peace,
no dignity,
no state,
no happiness,
no justice,
no hope
and no home
for them still
in any corners
of this world.

— Kaamil Ahmed, *I Feel No Peace*

Without you my Lord, I have no address.

— Message on t-shirt, opposite

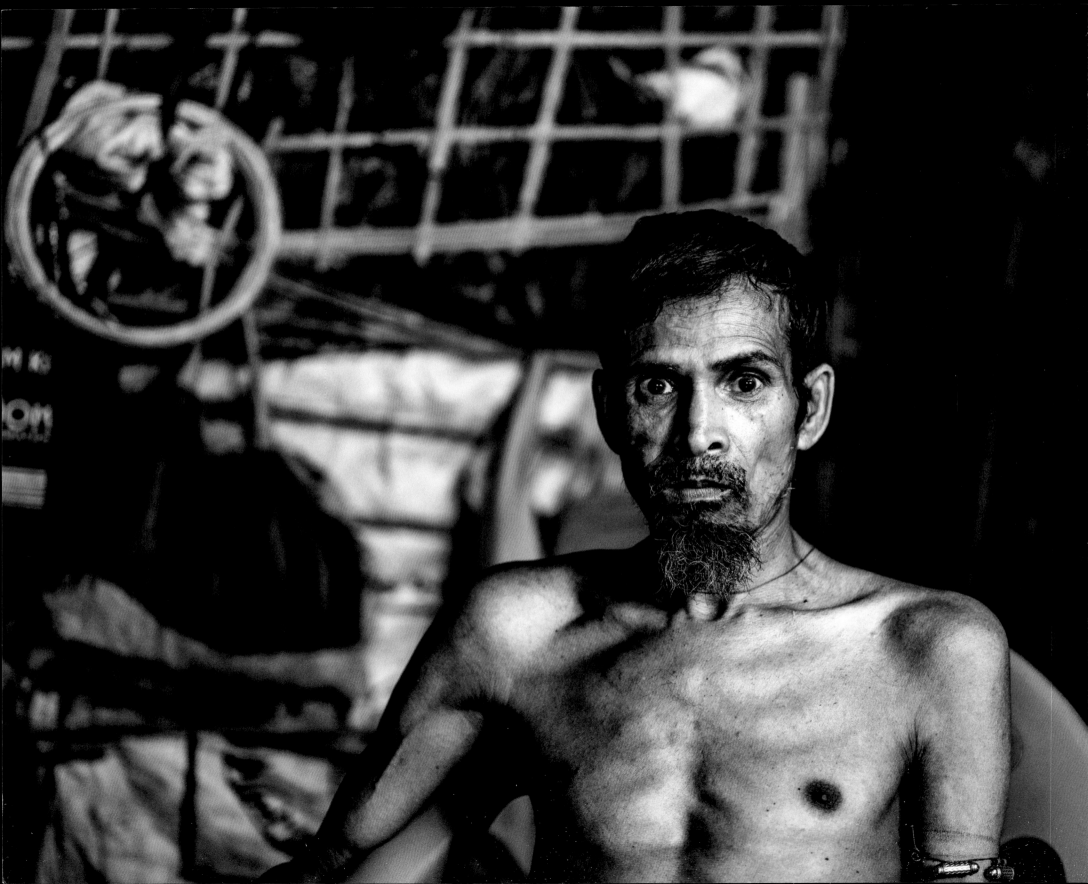

It was better to be home than to live as a stranger.

— Kaamil Ahmed, *I Feel No Peace*

Being illegal immigrants, they do not hold any immigration papers like the other nationals of the country.

— **Kaamil Ahmed,** *I Feel No Peace*

EDGE OF HOPE

A few lengths of rope
can be especially useful
— tied to planks of
wood to create floating
shelves for cooking
utensils, or attached to
hand-made cradles for
young babies that can
be gently rocked.

— Kaamil Ahmed

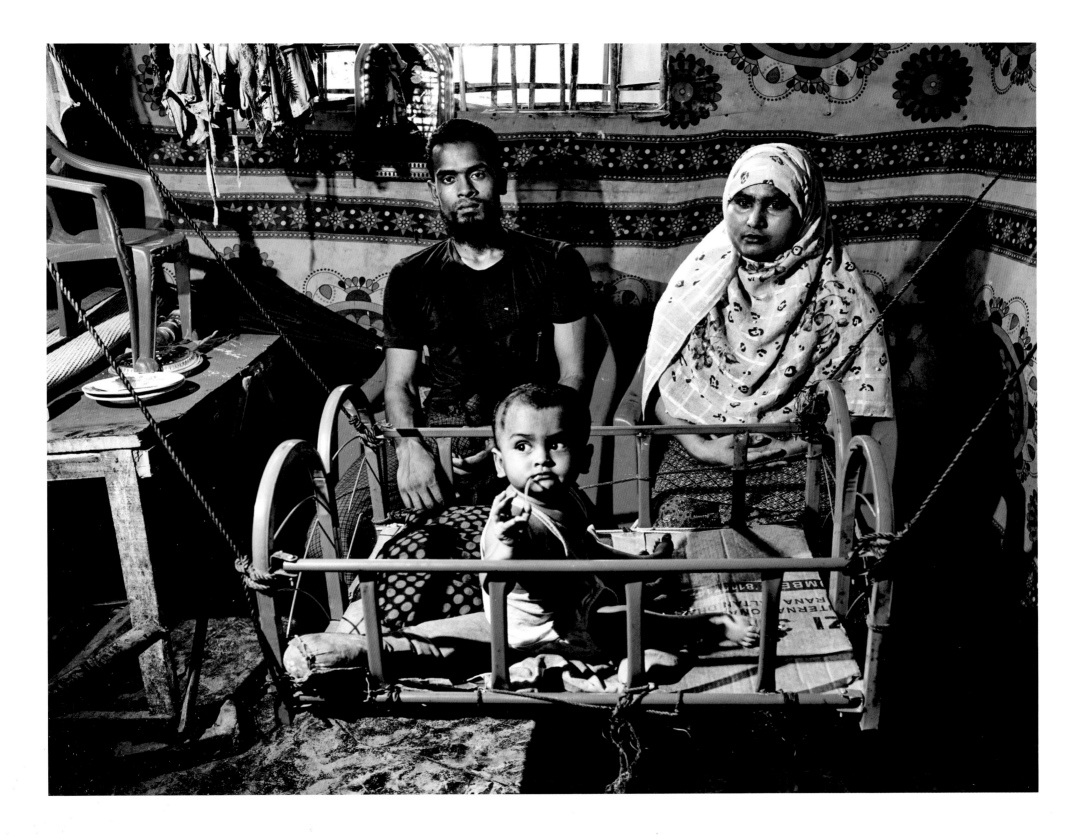

EDGE
OF
HOPE

Of those 900,000 refugees, more than 60% are children and here lies a very large problem waiting to arise.

— Dawton & McFarlane

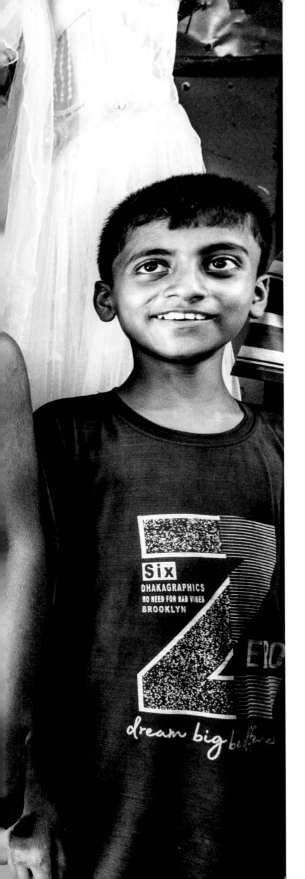

We want to go on talking and photographing because we have recognised again the humanity of a people who have nothing but will not give up.

— Dawton & McFarlane

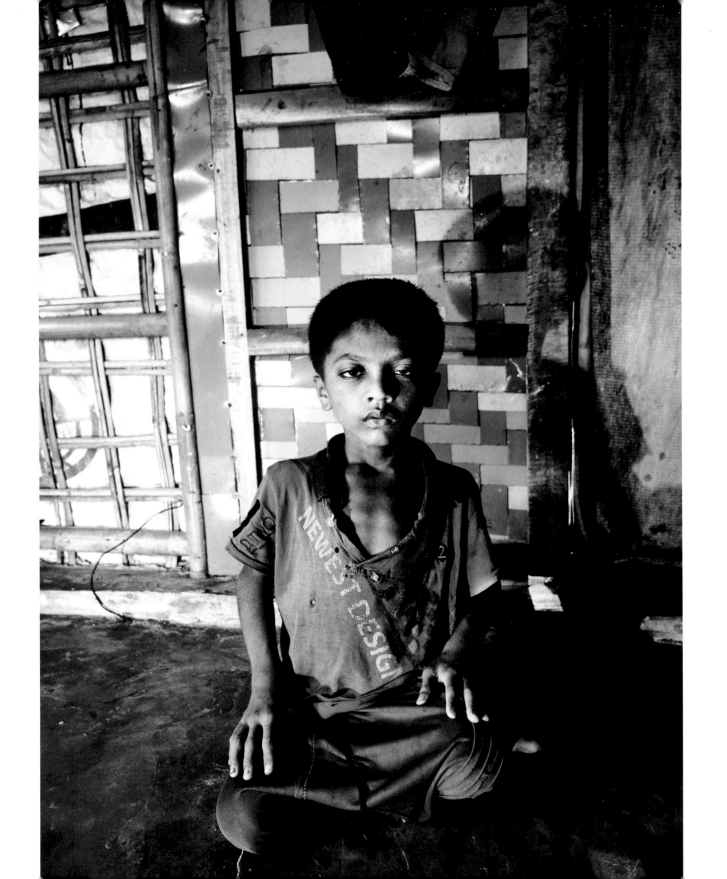

EDGE
OF
HOPE

DAWTON & McFARLANE

Dawton is an award-winning commercial photographer, having won the Fuji Industrial Photographer of the Year award, among others. His clients include Mercedes-Benz, J Walter Thompson, Tetrapak, the BBC and British Gas. His work has been published in the British newspapers *The Independent and The Guardian*. He was photographer-in-residence for the iconic arts magazine *Funoon Arabia*. His overseas clients have included the Monte Carlo Opera House, the Louvre, the Museum of Iraq, the Abha Festival in Saudi Arabia and Xenal Industries, Saudi Arabia, as well as the Government of Oman.

Dawton was one of six photographers featured in the Australian CCP exhibition that toured South-East Asia for 12 months in 2010. He has contributed to the Silent Witnesses book series: *Kashmir's Children, The Silent Witnesses of the Earthquake*, and *Desert Faces, The Silent Witnesses of the Niger Children*.

In September 2021 his book, *NotLondon*, was published. The result of nearly two years of photographing the homeless on the streets of London, the book has been greeted with critical acclaim.

Dawton lectures in London on photography and counts Lewis Hines, Eugene Smith, Bill Brandt, Michael Duane, Jim Goldberg and Jeffrey Wolin as important influences on his work and approach to photography.

McFarlane is an Australian-based photographer who has worked commercially for over 35 years. His expertise covers a wide range of subjects including food, dance, people and annual reports. McFarlane's food photography is seen on a vast range of food packaging and appeared in Melbourne's *Sunday Herald-Sun* every week for seven years.

The Australian Ballet has used McFarlane extensively for advertising and editorial work, including projects in China and Japan. He has been awarded by the Melbourne Art Director's Club and received the Oriental Fine Print award. Companies and organisations that have engaged him include BHP Billiton, Esso, Visa Card, Heinz, Edgell, Nestlé, McCormick Food, Birds Eye, John West, the Australian Opera, Leggo's, Mazda, Price Waterhouse and the National Bank.

McFarlane taught photography at Australia's leading art college, Deakin University, Melbourne, as well as the Victorian College of the Arts. His work is also included in the collection of the National Library of Australia.

Combined projects

Images from their UNICEF/Al Madad project in Niger were selected to show at the 2009 Sony World Photographic Awards, in Cannes.

In 2010 Dawton and McFarlane travelled to Gaza in the aftermath of the Israeli "incursion" the previous year, to photograph the effect on young people and the challenging landscape in which they and their families were living. Photographs taken during their time in Gaza formed a part of the Children of Gaza Exhibition project, which has so far raised more than $250,000 for Save the Children projects in Gaza.

In 2013 they entered what was then the largest refugee camp in the world, the camp in Zaatari, Jordan. The resulting images and film, known as the Hotel Zaatari Project, toured the Middle East as well as the UK.

In October 2014 the TMCP V.VC. Vorovsky factory in Tikhoretsk, Russia, invited Dawton and McFarlane to photograph the workers, continuing a tradition of recording the service given and the sacrifices made by the employees of the factory from before the time of the Soviet Revolution, from the Great War to the present day. An exhibition of the images taken opened at the TMCP factory in February 2015 and then transferred to Moscow.

Recent projects have been the photographing and filming of the Syrian refugee camps in the Bekka Valley, Lebanon, as well as in the Palestinian camps in Beirut. Exhibitions are planned for the US and the Middle East.

In May 2022 they photographed the flood-prone char islands in Bogra, Bangladesh, and spent eight days photographing in the Rohingya camp at Cox's Bazar for this publication.

Prints from this book are available for purchase.

Please visit — amalhopeproject.com

Dawton & McFarlane — Photographic Works
dawtonmcfarlane.com